# Putting
# Your Values
# On Paper™

# The Ethical Will Writing Guide Workbook

Barry K.Baines, M.D.

Preserving Your Legacy of Values
For
Your Family and Community

Published by Josaba Limited

1629 W. 25th St.

Minneapolis, MN 55405

612-374-9526

Printed in the United States of America

ISBN 0-9676794-1-9

# Table of Contents


| | |
|---|---|
| What is an Ethical Will | 1 |
| Why create an Ethical Will? | 2 |
| When might you write an Ethical Will? | 3 |
| How do you write an Ethical Will? | 4 |
| How to use the Ethical Will Writing Guide Workbook | 6 |
| Workbook Exercise | 7 |
| Next Steps | 25 |
| Resources | 26 |

# What is an Ethical Will?

An ethical will is a way to share with your family and community your

- Values
- Beliefs
- Life lessons
- Hopes for the future
- Love
- Forgiveness

Ethical wills are not new. The Hebrew Bible first described ethical wills 3000 years ago. They were first transmitted orally close to the time of death. Later they became written documents attached to legal wills. Today, they are most often written as a separate document and shared with family and community while the author is still alive.

# Why Create an Ethical Will?

People choose to write ethical wills for a variety of reasons (here is a list of them cited by participants in workshops and seminars I've conducted over the past few years):

- We all want to be remembered, and we all will leave something behind
- It helps identify what I value most and what I stand for
- By articulating what I value now, I can take steps to insure the continuation of those values for future generations
- I will learn a lot about myself in the process of writing an ethical will
- If I don't tell my stories and the stories from whom I come, no one else will and they will be lost forever
- It helps me to come to terms with my mortality by creating something of meaning that will live on after I am gone
- It provides a sense of completion to my life

# When Might You Write an Ethical Will?

People write ethical wills when facing challenging life situations and at different life stages. They are also being written as a foundation for estate planning by helping to articulate goals that are important to you.

Here are some transitional stages when writing an ethical will can be of great value:

- Betrothed Couples--for establishing a common base of values
- Expectant and new parents--to provide a framework for child-rearing
- Growing families--for teaching values to our children
- Empty-nesters--a time for reflection, providing advice, and hopes for success
- Middle age and beyond--converting life experience into wisdom and passing this on to future generations
- End of Life--adds to the transcendent dimension in our lives, the idea that you are part of something that goes beyond your lifetime

# How Do You Write an Ethical Will?

There are three basic approaches for writing an ethical will:

- Using an outline with items to choose from
- Using guided writing exercises
- Starting with a blank sheet of paper

The Ethical Will Writing Guide Workbook employs the first approach and can help you create a draft of your ethical will in a relatively short time.

This approach is helpful if you want something to go on right away, and a blank sheet of paper doesn't feel like an opportunity. In this workbook, you'll find 18 outline categories and several item choices in each category.

This may be one of the most valuable gifts you can give to your family and community.

# Beginning
# The
# Workbook Exercise

# How to use the Ethical Will Writing Guide Workbook

Read through the outline headings, e.g., Opening thoughts, Values and Beliefs, etc. Select as many of the items that resonate or speak to you. Feel free to change the wording by using the space provided below each phrase or sentence. Some of these items may stimulate and trigger your own thoughts. Write them down in the space at the bottom of each page. When you are finished, you can:

- Recopy your selections onto a blank sheet of paper to complete your first draft
- Return the workbook to the program or professional who gave this to you for conversion into a printed draft

# Opening thoughts

- ❑ To my unborn child: I am writing this in eager anticipation of your birth. I know that I have much to learn about being a parent.

- ❑ Dear Family and Friends: The following are the things that I have learned through life.

- ❑ Dear children: A few words to express my thoughts and feelings.

- ❑ To my family: In reading my ethical will, I hope you find few surprises.

- ❑ I want you, my family, to know how important you all are in my life and how much I love you.

- ❑ If you wish, record your own thoughts in the space below.

# Values and Beliefs

## Having Balance in Life

- Appreciate the importance of balance. Balance among the family, work, spiritual, and physical aspects of life.

- It's easy to let things get out of balance. When they do, life can get out of control and become miserable.

- The only way you can truly know yourself is to embrace life fully and in a balanced way.

- If you wish, record your own thoughts in the space below.

## The Importance of Education/Learning/Knowledge

- As long as you live you can always learn new things. This is an important value to cherish.

- It is a privilege to be able to share your knowledge and your love of learning with others.

- Read as if your life depended on it; it does.

- I tried and succeeded in giving my children a good education.

- I hope that you will have a passion for learning. In school, learn for the sake of learning and not with an eye only to a future career or how much money you can make.

- If you wish, record your own thoughts in the space below.

## The Importance of Family and Other Relationships

- ❑ As I've grown older I continue to value the family more and more.

- ❑ So much of what I am is because of Grandpa, and I dearly miss him every day.

- ❑ I had a special relationship with my grandmother. From her I learned that one should "do good for the sake of good, not for the sake of reward."

- ❑ I hope, especially for my family, to get along in life.

- ❑ If you find a good, true friend; hold on to him or her as hard as you can.

- ❑ If you wish, record your own thoughts in the space below.

## Being Honest, Truthful, and Sincere

- Be sincere yet decisive.

- Act as if all your actions will be part of a story published in the newspapers.

- I have always believed in honesty and advocated truthfulness.

- Be sincere and honest and learn to recognize these qualities in others. Call these people your friends.

- If you wish, record your own thoughts in the space below.

## The Importance of Humor

- ❑ Having a good sense of humor is very important.

- ❑ Keep a sense of humor.

- ❑ Humor ought to be a large part of every person's day.

- ❑ If you wish, record your own thoughts in the space below.

## Giving and Receiving

- In giving you make your life worthwhile.

- If you don't take, you will have nothing to give.

- Don't refuse to accept: others need a chance to give also.

- In sharing, one learns, experiences, and reaps the highest level of satisfaction.

- If you wish, record your own thoughts in the space below.

## Good

- Do good and avoid evil.

- Be aware of the evils of the world, but do not be consumed by them.

- I hope you will make the world a better place, both on a smaller scale and in the wider sense.

- If you wish, record your own thoughts in the space below.

## Learning From Your Mistakes

- ❑ Learn from mistakes. It's impossible to be successful in everything you try to do.

- ❑ Don't be afraid of making mistakes. Just be sure you learn something from them.

- ❑ You can learn more from a mistake than from always doing everything right.

- ❑ Don't fear mistakes, for mistakes are the springboard of future success.

- ❑ If you focus on things that are important to you, failures may come, but they will be fewer.

- ❑ If you wish, record your own thoughts in the space below.

## Having Respect for Life

- Respect life - yours and others. Treat other people the way you want to be treated.

- Be positive and look for the good in people.

- What is hateful to you do not do unto others.

- Cultivate a diverse group of friends and remember to judge a person as an individual, not by their ethnic, religious or racial group.

- If you wish, record your own thoughts in the space below.

**Religion/Spirituality**

- I hope you continue the traditions and faith of (fill in your faith community) and pass these on to future generations.

- My mission is to serve God by creating a balance between family, friends, profession, and community.

- I know I have never offered much in the way of spiritual guidance. However, I hope that my manner of living has served as a living example of my own moral code.

- Faith in God is important. I am not all that religious, but I am a believer.

- (Fill in your faith community) is your foundation but it is also important to be part of the larger world.

# Lessons and Reflections About Life

## Lessons

- Act on situations and opportunities, rather than be acted upon.

- Don't make assumptions of what people need. Ask them.

- Have a willingness to be open. You will learn more by listening than by speaking.

- Learn to be humble.

- Hard work and a broad understanding will bring success.

- If you wish, record your own thoughts in the space below.

## Reflections

- ❑ Remember that one person can make a difference.

- ❑ Stay true to yourself and give your best effort.

- ❑ Be courageous and persistent and accept differences.

- ❑ If you gauge your achievements on those of others, you will most likely be disappointed.

- ❑ Don't let yourselves be easily discouraged.

- ❑ If you wish, record your own thoughts in the space below.

# Hopes for the Future

- ❑ I hope that you can remember the good memories.

- ❑ I hope you are as lucky as I was in finding a soulmate like (name) to share your life with.

- ❑ Pursue your chosen path, study things that interest you, and use your college education to get you started.

- ❑ Try to be a part of the solution, not part of the problem.

- ❑ Keep before you for inspiration a vision of the way things ought to be, and help us move, albeit so slightly, in that direction.

- ❑ If you wish, record your own thoughts in the space below.

# Love

- My love for my grandchildren is too great to express in words. I hope I have expressed it in other ways.

- Show everyone that you love that you love him or her, and be sure to tell him or her as well.

- Be generous with love.

- To my precious family, I express my deep, unyielding love, for they were a great part of my life.

- No matter how lost or disconsolate you may seem at various points in your life, I hope this helps to bring you back on track: That your parents loved you intensely, unconditionally, and imaginatively.

- If you wish, record your own thoughts in the space below.

# Forgiveness

- ❑ I apologize for the times I wasn't the mom you would have liked.
- ❑ Never be afraid to say, "I'm sorry, please forgive me."
- ❑ Forgive whatever misunderstandings there are.
- ❑ Forgive me if I have hurt you in any way or if I have been too hard on you at times.
- ❑ If you wish, record your own thoughts in the space below.

# Requests

- Since no one can predict the future, I ask that should it ever be necessary, please see that your mother remains comfortable financially and otherwise.

- Enrich your mind, exercise your body, and feed your spirit with music, art, meaningful work, friends and helping the community at large.

- Be broad-minded and curious about the world.

- Try to find joy and beauty in the simple, ordinary things that life has to offer.

- Time is precious, do not waste it or take it for granted.

- If you wish, record your own thoughts in the space below.

# Concluding Thoughts

- You all have been a great source of joy and strength for me. I love you all very much.

- Finally, I am thankful for all those who have been good to me and have been helpful. I've learned to live a good life. I hope a good life for all. Goodbye.

- As I close here, I have to chuckle because I realize that even at the end of my life I do not stop giving directions. Humor me, it is who I am.

- My love will always be with you - you get to keep it and remember it forever.

- I love you all

- If you wish, record your own thoughts in the space below.

# Next Steps

Now that you've completed this exercise, you have an initial draft of your ethical will. Congratulations! You can revise and personalize this draft by adding your own stories, experiences, and other items of importance that will make your ethical will unique. When completed, write or print it on acid-free (archival) paper to improve the likelihood that your document will be preserved for many years to come.

The following pages list several resources and references that will provide you with additional ideas for creating your personal legacy of values.

## Software Resources

***_**Putting Your Values on Paper™: The Ethical Will Writing Guide**_ by Barry K. Baines MD and Wm. Bradley Rouse. Available for downloading or purchase at www.ethicalwll.com

## Internet Resources

**WWW.ETHICALWILL.COM**
More than 30 modern ethical wills are posted on this site.

## Organizational Resources

**The Legacy Center:** dedicated to preserving stories, values, and meaning for individuals, communities, and organizations. 1629 W. 25th St. Minneapolis, MN 55405, USA Tel: 612-333-2833 E-mail: thelegacycenter@aol.com
Web: www.thelegacycenter.net

## Books and Print Resources

*Ethical Wills: Putting your values on paper* by Barry K. Baines, MD, Perseus Publishing, 2002

*Women's Lives, Women's Legacies: Passing Your Beliefs and Blessings to Future Generations: Creating your spiritual-ethical will,* by Rachael Freed, Fairview Press, 2003.

*The Ethical Will Resource Kit*, by Barry K. Baines, M.D. Josaba Ltd. 1998

*So That Your Values Live On, Ethical Wills and How to Prepare Them* by Jack Riemer and Nathaniel Stampfer, Jewish Lights Publishing, 1991.

*Tuesday s With Morrie* by Mitch Albom, Doubleday, 1997

*Kitchen Table Wisdom,* by Rachel Naomi Remen, M.D. Riverhead Books, 1996.

*From Age-ing to Sage-ing*, by Zalman Schacther-Shalomi and Ronald Miller, Warner Books, 1997

*Man's Search for Meaning,* by Viktor Frankl, Simon and Schuster, 1959,1962,1984

*The Seven Habits of Highly Effective People*, by Stephen Covey, Simon and Schuster, published in 1989.

* Available at www.ethicalwill.com and at Brochin's Book and Gift Shop Tel: 952-926-2011 or toll-free 1-877-827-7323. Also available through Amazon.com.